Slow Cooker

100 Easy & Delicious Simple to Follow Slow Cooker Recipes

All In 3 Steps Or Less

By

NANCY KELSEY

Copyright © 2015 Nancy Kelsey

ISBN-13: 978-1514882337
ISBN-10: 1514882337

Copyright © 2015

Disclaimer

Table of Contents

Oatmeal Crock Pot

Crock Pot Lemon Chicken

Crock Pot Corned Beef and Cabbage

Crock Pot Beef Vegetable Soup

Crock Pot Teriyaki Steak

Easy Crock Pot Pork Roast

Hamburger Barley Stew

Crock Pot Meatloaf

Crock Pot Rice Pudding

Slow-Cooker Cajun Chicken Pasta

Slow Cooker Beef Stroganoff

Slow Cooker Chops

Beef Barley Veggy Soup

Slow Cooker Pork Tenderloin

Crock Pot Posole

Crock Pot Apricot Chicken

Crock Pot Green Beans

Country Style Ribs

Slow Cooker Enchilada Casserole

Crock Pot Rigatoni

Crock Pot Applesauce

Japanese Beef Stew

Crock Pot Bean Dip

Crock Pot Baked Beans Bananza

Crock-Pot Macaroni and Cheese

Drunken Meatballs

Crock Pot Cranberry Chicken

Slow Cooker Chicken Dinner

Turkey Leg Pot Roast

Crock Pot Pork Loin

Easy Potato and Corn Chowder

Pepperoncini Crock Pot Beef

Baked Cinnamon Apples

Mushroom Pork Tenderloin

Crock Pot Chicken Paprika

Slow-Cooker Steak Chili

Hamburger Vegetable Soup - Crock Pot

Crock Pot Taco Dip

Vegetarian Slow Cooker Split Pea Soup

Crock Pot Creamy Ranch Chicken Light

Easy Crock Pot BBQ Chicken (Low Fat)

Tangy Slow Cooker Pork Roast

Beef & Baked Beans Stew

Crock Pot Breakfast Apple Cobbler

Slow Cooker Lasagna

Crock Pot Pepperoni Pizza Dip

Crock Pot Clam Chowder

Cabbage and Sausage Crock Pot

Crock Pot Beef Stew

Vegetable-Beef Barley Soup

Crock Pot Chicken Cacciatore

Crock Pot Chicken Vegetable Soup

Crock Pot Roast

Vegetarian meat Filling Substitute

Crock Pot Chicken Fajitas

Slow Cooker Lentils

Sweet Crock Pot Chicken

Crock Pot Pizza

Meat Loaf With Shiitake Mushrooms

Crock Pot Spinach Special

Tomato Soup With Israeli Couscous

Vegetarian Chipotle Chili

Tomato Spinach Slow Cooker Soup

Broccoli Cheese Soup for the Crock Pot

Crock Pot Creamy Chicken

Easy Crock Pot Meatballs

Crock Pot Melt

Crock Pot Blueberry Dump Cake

Split Pea and Parsnip Soup

INTRODUCTIONS :-

Hearty thanks and congratulations to all of you who have been successful in downloading the most eagerly awaited book *Slow Cooker*. The content comprises of some proven steps along with strategies regarding the best possible methods to make slow cooking highly efficient and simple.

Recent observations have revealed that slow cooking is becoming very much popular for its convenience in bringing out each and every busy family out there. It is also considered to be a stepping stone for guys who prefer learning more about cooking but have not at all figured out the starting stone yet.

It is universal truth that that cooking a delicious homemade meal tastes better than the opened and artificially boiled cheese and mac. It has also been considered to comprise of:

- Healthier
- Easier
- Convenient way of cooking.

All have been made possible by the magic of slow cooking! People usually keep themselves engaged in preparing a healthier and tastier dish for themselves.

Visiting restaurants has been considered to be an upsetting factor for money bag. Also, consumption of too much of fast food will result in running a person to the emergency room of nearby clinic due to serious health condition.

In order to avoid such unexpected mishaps, preparing a healthy as well as convenient meal is the dire need of the hour! For that, the only key is employing Slow Cooker or Crock-Pot. In case you are among those people devoid of any clues regarding the art of slow cooking, it is high time to take out time to read between the lines.

The book published with due care will be providing you algorithmic guidance about the methodology associated with slow cooking along with providing the best ideas regarding the basic ingredients essential of preparing any selected dish. Easy to learn the basics for proper starting! Some other benefits you can expect from this book include:

- *Learning of magical techniques for maximizing the benefits of slow cooking*
- *Best suitable ingredients to be added*
- *Tips and tricks to optimize the task in kitchen*
- *Easy to make recipes providing culinary experience*

Initially, you will be gifted with some valuable pages which include some ingredient dishes which will be worth for busy guys. Also you will be taught about the dos and don'ts along with maximizing the budget while selecting specific ingredients. Also you will be provided with a couple of safe reminders that are mandatory for safe cooking.

Thank you once again for downloading this hardback! Hope it will make you interesting!

HISTORY SLOW COOKER

Knowing about some Historical facts will make slow cooking highly interesting! The Naxon Beanery all-purpose Cooker was developed by the Naxon Utilities Corporation which was under the headship of Irving Naxon in Chicago. Naxon got stimulated through a small story recited by his grandmother. He was informed about the ways her mother prepared *cholent* a stew in Lithuanian Shtetl.

As the cooking took place in a stove, it took long to get prepared. One day in 1970, The Rival Company purchased Naxon and reintroduced the same by the name Crock-Pot by 1971. During the 1970s, slow cookers received high status in the United States when ladies started to work outside the home. They were successful in cooking their dinner by starting in the morning before going out and concluded successfully in the twilight after coming back home.

In the mid-session Rival initiated removal of stoneware inserts by 1974, which proved to be highly convenient for cleaning of the appliance. At present, the brand is in favor of *Sunbeam Products* which is an ancillary of *Jarden Corporation*. Some other brands for this sppliance include:

- *Hamilton Beach*
- *West Bend Housewares*
- *GE*
- *Magic Chef*
- *Kitchen Aid Cuisinart*
- *American Electric Corporation*

Advantages of Slow Cooking

In case you are a lover of non vegetarian or varieties of food items, then slow cooking can be considered to be highly beneficial. Some of the associated benefits of slow cooking can be stated in a nutshell as under:

- Slow cooking will leave the gelatinized tissue in the meat itself. It will also make the connective bandanna of meats softer without strengthening the fiber of lean muscle. You may also use a more affluent juice for smooth stewing process.

- Even if you go for long cooking, you need not fear about getting your food item getting burned due to the presence of low temperature. But try to avoid the consequence of overcooking as it may leave the food tasteless.

- You can set the food item to cooking before leaving and get ready on reaching back after the hectic schedule of entire day. Also, it will consume low power due to presence of grid. In case there is a solar panel in the house, then relax!

- Catering the snack in a solitary jar will prevent wastage of water which takes place while washing of multiple dishes. At the same time squat temperature for food preparation of glazed pot will make cleaning easier in comparison to conventional pots.

Shortcomings of Slow Cooking that Can be Prevented with Due Care

Apart from fetching high rated benefits associated with the process of slow cooking, there are some negative points regarding the same as well. But they can be prevented if you are a bit careful. They can be stated as under:

- Due to enzyme action and partial heat degradation in slow cooking, some vitamins along with traces of additional nutrients get lost. In case of cooking at high temperature, the enzymes get denatured in a rapid manner and holds less time.
- As slow cookers are known to work under estimated scorching dot, they are not successful in rapid denaturing of enzymes due to which vegetables suffer loss of traces of some nutrients. Blanching pre-cooked phase will depart higher traces of vitamins intact which can be prevented by not disturbing the cover in anticipation of the cooking has been done.
- Due to frequent removal of lead, slow cookers are not able to supply adequate warmth for the

process of compensating defeat of dampness and warm up. Additional components must be provided due time to get cooked before consumption which becomes quite impossible in case of slow cookers. It results in the growth of harmful bacteria which do not get destroyed even after reheating.

THEN WHY TO PURCHASE A SLOW COOKER?

If you are still wondering why to go for a slow cooker, then listen! It can be easily considered to be a convenient and among the easiest ways of preparing a delicious meal. It will also assist in reducing costs as the cheaper cuts of meat are perfect match for slow cookers. They are known to get tenderized during the process of slow cooking.

In case you plan to enjoy a delicious meal after coming back from a visit in the garden or friends all day long, it will be the best possible alternate. The slow cookers will prove to be a boon for mums busy with their small and cute children. Almost all types of recipes can be adapted in case of a slow cooker.

Points to Ponder while Choosing of a Selective Slow Cooker

If you are planning to purchase a smart slow cooker for your home, then do not think twice before running to a retail shop dealing with the same. You may also go for online shopping portals. But before making the purchase, it is advised to keep some vital points in due considerations which are:

- *The amount of food that the slow cooker can hold* - Generally almost all slow cookers hold a good capacity but usually the cooking space is two-thirds of the actual mentioned space. Hence, for bulk cooking, six liters will be the best. Otherwise, 3-3.5 liters is enough. You may also refer to the cooker comparison tool for convenience.

- *Cooking of whole or partial chicken* - It is a vital point to consider in case you prefer chicken dishes. In case you plan to cook stews or curries, then round shaped slow cookers will serve you the best.

- *Inclusion of smart timer controls* – In case you hold a good finance to spend, then you may go for slow cookers which include smart timer controls within them. The inclusion of an indicator will inform you about the on and off status of the cooker. For further details, refer the section of *slow cookers features explained*.

RECIPES FOR SLOW COOKER

No need to worry in case you are new to the world of cooking as maximum slow cooker is included with a recipe book. In case that is not present, you will be provided with the instruction manual. If you are a computer savvy, then you may go for browsing the internet.

But keep in mind that while cooking in a slow cooker, you need to reduce the amount of liquid used as it is hoped that you are familiar with the vital causes. Following the instruction manual in a religious manner will let you learn proper usage of the cooker along with letting you know the actual amount of liquid required for cooking.

ADDITIONAL RECIPES TO BE PREPARED IN SLOW COOKER

The usage of slow cookers is not only limited to soups, stews and casseroles. If you hold a little bit of interest in the field of cooking, you may easily try the following dishes:

- Lasagne
- Homemade stock along with left over roast chicken carcass
- Deserts
- Mulled Wine and many more.

For further inspiration and suggestions, go through the which? Conversation on slow cooker recipes section!

Slow-Cooker Creamy Chicken

- **Prep Time:** 5 mins
- **Total Time:** 5 mins
- **Servings:** 4

Ingredients

- 1 1/2 lbs boneless skinless chicken breasts
- 10 1/2 ounces Healthy Request cream of chicken soup
- 8 ounces low-fat cream cheese or 8 ounces fat free cream cheese
- 1 (2/3 ounce) package Good Seasonings Italian salad dressing mix
- 6 ounces mushrooms (optional)

Directions

1. Mix all ingredients in a crock pot.
2. Cook them on low heat for an entire day.
3. Serve hot with brown rice or w/w pasta.

Slow Cooker Pot Roast

- **Prep Time:** 10 mins
- **Total Time:** 8 hrs 10 mins
- **Servings:** 12

Ingredients

- 2 (10 3/4 ounce) cans condensed cream of mushroom soup
- 1 (1 ounce) package dry onion soup mix
- 1 1/4 cups water
- 5 1/2 lbs pot roast

Directions

1. Mix dry onion soup mix, cream of mushroom soup and water together in a slow cooker.
2. Coat the pot roast with soup mixture and place it in the slow cooker.
3. Cook it for 3 to 4 hours on High setting, or for 8 to 9 hours on Low setting.

BEEF ROAST

- **Prep Time:** 10 mins
- **Total Time:** 3 hrs 10 mins
- **Servings:** 6

Ingredients :-

- 2 lbs beef roast
- 4 potatoes, peeled and cut into 1-inch cubes
- 1 1/2 cups baby carrots
- 1 large onion, quartered and pulled apart
- 1 1/2 cups beef broth
- 1 (1 1/2 ounce) envelopes dry vegetable soup mix (I use Knorr)

Directions :-

1. Surround the roast with vegetables and place it into crock pot.
2. Mix vegetable soup mix and beef broth together and add it to the crock pot.
3. Put the lid on it and cook for 6 to8 hours on LOW setting or 3 to 4 hours on HIGH setting.

CROCK POT CANDY

- **Prep Time:** 5 mins
- **Total Time:** 2 hrs 5 mins
- **Servings:** 24

Ingredients :-

- 1 (16 ounce) packages dry roasted salted peanuts
- 1 (16 ounce) packages unsalted dry roasted peanuts
- 1 (12 ounce) packages semi-sweet chocolate bits
- 1 (4 ounce) German chocolate bars
- 32 ounces white almond bark

Directions :-

1. Place the peanuts at the bottom of the crock pot.
2. Put the rest of the ingredients.
3. Cook it for 1 1/2 to 2 hours on low setting.
4. Place the crock pot onto wax paper and let it cool down.

Chicken & Dumplings

- **Prep Time:** 10 mins
- **Total Time:** 5 hrs 10 mins
- **Servings:** 5

Ingredients :-

- 2 cups chopped cooked chicken
- 1 (10 3/4 ounce) cans cream of mushroom soup, undiluted
- 1 (10 3/4 ounce) cans cream of chicken soup, undiluted
- 2 (10 3/4 ounce) soup cans water
- 4 teaspoons all-purpose flour
- 2 teaspoons chicken bouillon granules
- 1/2 teaspoon black pepper
- 1 (8 count) packages refrigerated buttermilk biscuits

Directions :-

1. Combine all ingredients together except for the biscuits in the Crock pot.
2. Break the biscuits into quarters and slowly stir them into mixture.
3. Put the lid on it to cook for 4 to 6 hours on low heat setting.

Low-Carb Slow Cooker Crock Pot

- **Prep Time:** 5 mins
- **Total Time:** 8 hrs 5 mins
- **Serves:** 6, **Yield:** 1 Pot

Ingredients

- cooking spray
- 1 small head of cabbage, cored and cut into wedges (about 2 1/2 lbs)
- 1 medium onion, halved and thinly sliced
- 1/2 teaspoon kosher salt
- 1/2 teaspoon black pepper
- 1 cup chicken broth
- 1 tablespoon brown mustard
- 1 lb kielbasa, cut into 3-inch pieces

Directions

1. With cooking spray, coat the slow cooker crock pot. Put all the ingredients to the crock except for the kielbasa.
2. Toss them so that the broth and seasonings coat the cabbage well.
3. Put the kielbasa on top. Cover it with lid and cook it on LOW for 7 hours. Give the mixture a good stir, and cook it for 1 more hour.

Slow Cooker Stuffing

- **Prep Time:** 5 mins
- **Total Time:** 6 hrs 5 mins
- **Servings:** 12

Ingredients :-

- 1 cup butter
- 2 cups chopped celery
- 1 cup chopped onion
- 1 teaspoon poultry seasoning
- 1 1/2 teaspoons sage leaves, crumbled
- 1/2 teaspoon pepper
- 1 1/2 teaspoons salt
- 1 teaspoon leaf thyme, crumbled
- 2 beaten eggs
- 4 cups chicken broth
- 12 cups dry breadcrumbs

Directions :-

1. Combine the celery, butter, eggs, spices and the broth together in a large mixing bowl and mix them well.
2. Stir the bread crumbs into this.
3. Cook it for 45 minutes in slow cooker on high heat setting.
4. After 45 minutes, reduce the heat to low and cook for another 6 hours.

Ratatouille With Chickpeas

- **Prep Time:** 15 mins
- **Total Time:** 4 hrs 15 mins
- **Serves:** 6, **Yield:** 6

Ingredients

- 1 tablespoon vegetable oil
- 1 onion, chopped
- 4 garlic cloves, minced
- 6 cups eggplants, cubed (one large)
- 2 teaspoons basil (dried)
- 1 teaspoon oregano (dried)
- 1/2 teaspoon salt
- 1/2 teaspoon pepper
- 1 red pepper
- 1 yellow pepper
- 2 zucchini
- 1/3 cup tomato paste
- 1 (19 ounce) cans chickpeas, drained and rinsed
- 1 (28 ounce) cans tomatoes
- 1/4 cup fresh basil or 1/4 cup fresh parsley, chopped

Directions

1. Heat oil over medium heat in a large skillet. Cook onion, garlic and eggplant in it, with basil,

oregano, salt & pepper seasonings. Keep stirring occasionally for about 10 minutes, so that the onion is softened. Scrape this into the crock pot.

2. Cut the peppers into 1 inch pieces after halving, coring, and deseeding them. Cut zucchini first into half lengthwise and then crosswise into 1 1/2 inch chunks. Add them to the crock pot.

3. Stir in the tomato paste, tomatoes, and chickpeas. Make sure that you break up the tomatoes with a spoon. Cover the crock pot and cook for 4 hours on low, or until vegetables are tender. Add the basil / parsley at the end.

CROCK POT ROUND STEAK

- **Prep Time:** 5 mins
- **Total Time:** 6 hrs 5 mins
- **Servings:** 4-6

Ingredients

- 2 -3 lbs round steaks
- 1 (1 1/4 ounce) envelopes dry onion soup mix
- 2 (10 1/2 ounce) cans cream of mushroom soup
- 1 (8 ounce) jars mushrooms
- 1/4 cup water

Directions

1. Mix all ingredients in a crock pot.
2. Cook for 8-10 hours on low or for 5-6 hours on high.
3. Serve with mashed potatoes.

CROCK POT CARAMELIZED ONIONS

- **Prep Time:** 6 mins
- **Total Time:** 10 hrs 6 mins
- **Serves:** 12, **Yield:** 3 cups

Ingredients

- 3 lbs sliced onions
- 1/2 cup melted margarine (or butter)
- 1 teaspoon salt

Directions

1. Mix margarine, onions and salt in a crock pot.
2. Cover it with a lid and cook for 8-10 hours on low.

PORK CHOPS FOR THE SLOW COOKER

- **Prep Time:** 5 mins
- **Total Time:** 6 hrs 5 mins
- **Servings:** 6

Ingredients

- 6 boneless pork chops
- 1/4 cup brown sugar
- 1 teaspoon ground ginger
- 1/2 cup soy sauce
- 1/4 cup ketchup
- 2 garlic cloves, Crushed
- salt & pepper

Directions

1. In a slow cooker place the pork chops.
2. Add all the remaining ingredients to it and pour over the pork chops.
3. Cook for 6 hours on Low setting, or until the internal temperature of the pork reaches 160 degrees F.

CROCK POT CREAM CORN

- **Prep Time:** 10 mins
- **Total Time:** 4 hrs 10 mins
- **Servings:** 6-8

Ingredients

- 20 ounces frozen corn
- 1/2 cup oleo
- 1 (8 ounce) packages cream cheese
- 1 1/2 tablespoons sugar

Directions

1. Cook all ingredients together for about 4 hours on low heat setting in a crock pot.
2. Keep stirring them occasionally, until all the ingredients are well blended.
3. If you are using a large crock pot, triple the amount of all the ingredients.

EASY CROCK POT ROAST BEEF

- **Prep Time:** 5 mins
- **Total Time:** 10 hrs 5 mins
- **Servings:** 6

Ingredients

- 2 lbs beef roast (any cut will work, whatever is on sale)
- 1 (10 1/4 ounce) cans French onion soup

- 1 (10 1/4 ounce) cans cream of mushroom soup
- 3/4 cup dry red wine
- 6 ounces fresh mushrooms, sliced

Directions

1. Mix all the ingredients into a crock pot and cook for 8-10 hours set on low heat setting.
2. It would make a great base for gravy if you use the juice and soup with some flour. Add flour until the correct consistency of the gravy is reached.

CROCK POT MAPLE

- **Prep Time:** 10 mins
- **Total Time:** 6 hrs 10 mins
- **Servings:** 4

Ingredients

- 3 lbs country-style pork ribs (western style work too)
- 1 cup maple syrup
- 1/2 cup applesauce
- 1/4 cup ketchup

- 3 tablespoons lemon juice
- 1/4 teaspoon salt
- 1/4 teaspoon pepper
- 1/4 teaspoon paprika
- 1/4 teaspoon garlic powder
- 1/4 teaspoon ground cinnamon

Directions

1. Combine everything together in your crock pot and cook for 6-8 hours on low heat setting.

CROCK POT THAI CHICKEN THIGHS

- **Prep Time:** 5 mins
- **Total Time:** 6 hrs 5 mins
- **Servings:** 4

Ingredients

- 8 boneless skinless chicken thighs
- 1 (16 ounce) jars cilantro salsa (or any salsa you prefer)
- 1/2 cup peanut butter (crunchy or creamy)
- 2 teaspoons ginger
- 2 tablespoons soy sauce
- 2 teaspoons lime juice

Directions

1. Combine all ingredients together for 6-8 hours on low heat setting in a crock pot.
2. Garnish with scallions, cilantro and peanuts.
3. Serve hot with jasmine rice.

OATMEAL CROCK POT

- **Prep Time:** 5 mins
- **Total Time:** 6 hrs 5 mins
- **Servings:** 3-4

Ingredients

- 1 cup steel cut oats (DO NOT substitute old-fashioned or quick-cooking oats)
- 4 1/2 cups water
- 1/2 teaspoon salt
- 2 -3 tablespoons butter
- 1/2 cup dried fruit (raisins, prunes, apricots, dates) (optional)

Serve with

- milk, to taste
- sugar, to taste
- cinnamon, to taste

- maple syrup, to taste

Directions

1. Mix everything together in a 2 quart slow cooker. You can use a smaller crock pot or crockette to make the dish in small portion.
2. Cover the lid and cook for 6-8 hours on LOW.
3. Scrape the crust down, if any formed, with a spoon and stir.

CROCK POT LEMON CHICKEN

- **Prep Time:** 15 mins
- **Total Time:** 8 hrs 15 mins
- **Servings:** 4

Ingredients

- 1 (3 lb) broiler-fryer chickens (whole or pieces)
- 1 teaspoon crumbled dry oregano
- 1/2 teaspoon crumbled dried rosemary
- 3 garlic cloves, minced
- 2 tablespoons butter
- 1/4 cup sherry wine or 1/4 cup chicken broth
- 1/4 cup lemon juice

- salt and pepper

Directions

1. After washing the chicken season it generously with half of the oregano, rosemary, garlic and salt and pepper inside cavity of the chicken. Melt butter in a frying pan and brown the chicken. Put the chicken in a slow cooker or crock pot and sprinkle with remaining rosemary, oregano and garlic. Add sherry to the frying pan and loosen the brown bits from chicken.
2. Pour this into the slow cooker. Put the lid on and cook for 7 hours on LOW heat (200 degrees).
3. Then add the lemon juice and cook for another 1 hour. Slice the chicken by putting it on a chopping board, skim fat from the juices and serve over the sliced chicken.

CROCK POT CORNED BEEF AND CABBAGE

- **Prep Time:** 5 mins
- **Total Time:** 10 hrs 5 mins
- **Servings:** 4-6

Ingredients

- 4 1/2 lbs corned beef brisket

- 2 medium onions, quartered
- 1 head cabbage, cut in small wedges
- 1/2 teaspoon pepper
- 3 tablespoons vinegar
- 3 tablespoons sugar
- 2 cups water

Directions

1. Mix all ingredients in a crock pot with the cabbage on top.
2. Cover with lid and cook for 10-12 hours on low; 6-7 hours on high or 6-8 hours on auto mode.

CROCK POT BEEF VEGETABLE SOUP

- **Prep Time:** 20 mins
- **Total Time:** 8 hrs 20 mins
- **Servings:** 6

Ingredients

- 1 lb boneless round steak, cubed
- 1 (14 ounce) cans diced tomatoes, do not drain
- 24 fluid ounces beef broth
- 3 beef bouillon cubes
- 2 medium potatoes, peeled and cubed

- 2 medium onions, chopped
- 2 celery ribs, sliced
- 2 carrots, chopped
- 1/2 teaspoon basil
- 1/2 teaspoon oregano
- 1/2 teaspoon thyme
- 1 bay leaf
- 1/4 teaspoon pepper
- 1 cup fresh peas or 1 cup frozen peas

Directions

1. Put all the ingredients in the rock pot.
2. Put the lid and cook for 7-8 hours on low.
3. Remove bay leaf and serve.

CROCK POT TERIYAKI STEAK

- **Prep Time:** 10 mins
- **Total Time:** 6 hrs 10 mins
- **Servings:** 4-6

Ingredients

- 2 -2 1/2 lbs boneless sirloin steaks, cut up in small pieces
- 1 teaspoon ginger
- 1 tablespoon sugar

- 2 tablespoons vegetable oil
- 1/2 cup soy sauce
- 2 garlic cloves, crushed

Directions

1. Mix all ingredients and put them over the steak.
2. Cook in crock pot for 4 to 6 hours on low.
3. Serve with rice.

EASY CROCK POT PORK ROAST

- **Prep Time:** 5 mins
- **Total Time:** 8 hrs 5 mins
- **Servings:** 8

Ingredients

- 1 (4 lb) boneless pork roast
- 3 -4 garlic cloves, chopped
- 1 tablespoon A.1. Original Sauce
- 1 teaspoon fresh ground pepper
- 1 small onion, sauteed
- 2 (10 1/2 ounce) cans cream of mushroom soup

Directions

1. Mix all ingredients in crock-pot.
2. Add the roast and coat with this.
3. Cook for 8 hours on low or for 4 hours on high.

HAMBURGER BARLEY STEW

- **Prep Time:** 15 mins
- **Total Time:** 5 hrs 15 mins
- **Servings:** 10-12

Ingredients

- 1 lb extra lean ground beef, browned
- 5 cups water
- 3 (14 ounce) cans tomatoes seasoned with basil garlic & oregano, with juice
- 3 cups sliced carrots
- 1 cup diced celery
- 1 cup diced potato
- 1 cup diced onion
- 3/4 cup pearl barley, rinsed
- 3 teaspoons beef bouillon granules or 3 beef bouillon cubes
- 1 teaspoon salt
- 1/4 teaspoon pepper

Directions

1. Dissolve bouillon in water.

2. In the slow cooker mix all ingredients.
3. Put lid on and cook for 9-10 hours on low or for 4.5-5 hours on high.

CROCK POT MEATLOAF

- **Prep Time:** 10 mins
- **Total Time:** 3 hrs 10 mins
- **Servings:** 6

Ingredients

- 2 eggs, beaten
- 3/4 cup milk
- 3/4 cup dry breadcrumbs
- 1 (1 ounce) envelope dry onion soup mix
- 2 lbs lean ground beef

Directions

1. Line the crock pot with wide strip of aluminum foil so that the loaf comes out easily from the sides of the crock.
2. Mix eggs, bread crumbs, milk and soup mix. Stir in the meat and mix thoroughly.Give it a rectangle or oval shape so that it doesn't touch the sides of crock.

3. Place it in the crock.Put the lid and cook for 6 hours on low or for 3 hours on high.

CROCK POT RICE PUDDING

- **Prep Time:** 5 mins
- **Total Time:** 5 hrs 5 mins
- **Servings:** 8

Ingredients

- 3/4 cup short-grain rice
- 1 (13 1/2 ounce) cans evaporated milk (skim is fine, 385ml)
- 2 cups water
- 1/3 cup white sugar
- 1/2 cup raisins
- 1 1/2 teaspoons vanilla
- 3/4 teaspoon salt
- 1 (3 inch) cinnamon sticks

Directions

1. Mix all ingredients in slow cooker.
2. Put the lid and cook for 4 to 5 hours on Low or for 2 to 2-1/2 hours on High.
3. Stir only twice.

SLOW-COOKER CAJUN CHICKEN PASTA

- **Prep Time:** 15 mins
- **Total Time:** 3 hrs 15 mins
- **Servings:** 4-6

Ingredients

- 1 1/2 lbs boneless skinless chicken breasts, cut into bite-size pieces
- 1 (16 ounce) jars alfredo sauce (book recommends Classico)
- 1 (14 1/2 ounce) cans diced tomatoes, undrained (with green pepper celery and onion)
- 1 (14 ounce) cans reduced-sodium chicken broth (Recommend leaving out, makes too sauce runny) (optional)
- 1 medium red bell pepper, cut into strips
- 4 teaspoons cajun seasoning
- 1 lb dry bow tie pasta
- fresh chives, chopped (optional)

Directions

1. Mix chicken, tomatoes and juices, alfredo sauce, chicken broth, cajun seasoning and peppers in the slow-cooker.

2. Put the lid and cook for 3-4 hours on HIGH, or for 6-8 hours on LOW.
3. Serve chicken with pasta with the sauce over the cooked pasta. Garnish with chives.

Slow Cooker Beef Stroganoff

- **Prep Time:** 10 mins
- **Total Time:** 8 hrs 10 mins
- **Servings:** 4

Ingredients

- 1 lb beef stew meat
- 1/2 cup chopped onion
- 2 (10 3/4 ounce) cans condensed cream condensed golden mushroom soup or 2 (10 3/4 ounce) cans regular cream of mushroom soup
- 1 (4 ounce) cans sliced mushrooms, drained
- 1/4 teaspoon pepper
- 1 cup sour cream
- 3 cups hot cooked noodles or 3 cups cooked rice

Directions

1. Mix onion, beef, mushrooms, soup and pepper in a 2 1/2- to 3 1/2-quart slow cooker.
2. Put the lid and cook for 8 to 10 hours on low heat setting to make the beef tender.
3. Add the sour cream into the beef mixture. Serve with noodles.

SLOW COOKER CHOPS

- **Prep Time:** 5 mins
- **Total Time:** 8 hrs 5 mins
- **Servings:** 4

Ingredients

- 4 pork chops
- 1 can condensed cream of mushroom soup
- 1/4 cup ketchup
- 2 teaspoons Worcestershire sauce

Directions

1. Put the pork chops at the bottom of a crock pot.
2. Pour all other ingredients over chops.
3. Cook for 8-10 hours on low or for 3-4 hours on high.

BEEF BARLEY VEGGY SOUP

- **Prep Time:** 20 mins
- **Total Time:** 9 hrs 20 mins
- **Servings:** 10-12

Ingredients

- 1 1/2 lbs beef stew meat
- 1 cup green beans, sliced in half
- 3/4 cup chopped onion
- 2/3 cup uncooked barley
- 2/3 cup fresh frozen corn kernels or 2/3 cup fresh frozen corn kernels
- 1 cup chopped celery
- 1 cup bias sliced carrot
- 1 1/2 cups water
- 1 teaspoon salt
- 1 teaspoon chopped fresh thyme leaves or 1/2 teaspoon dried thyme leaves
- 1/4 teaspoon pepper
- 1 small bell pepper, chopped
- 2 (14 1/2 ounce) cans ready-to-serve beef broth
- 2 (14 1/2 ounce) cans diced tomatoes with garlic, undrained
- 1 (8 ounce) cans tomato sauce

Directions

1. Mix everything together in a 4-5 quart slow cooker crock pot.
2. Put the lid and cook for 8-9 hours on low setting until veggies and barley become soft.

SLOW COOKER PORK TENDERLOIN

- **Prep Time:** 15 mins
- **Total Time:** 4 hrs 15 mins
- **Servings:** 8

Ingredients

- 2 lbs pork tenderloin
- 1 (1 ounce) envelope dry onion soup mix
- 1 cup water
- 3/4 cup red wine
- 3 tablespoons minced garlic
- 3 tablespoons soy sauce
- fresh ground black pepper

Directions

1. Place pork tenderloin and empty contents of the soup packet in a slow cooker. Add water, soy sauce and wine over, to coat the pork.

2. Spread garlic and pepper over the pork during cooking. Cook for 4 hours on low setting.
3. Serve with the cooking liquid as au jus.

CROCK POT POSOLE

- **Prep Time:** 30 mins
- **Total Time:** 5 hrs 30 mins
- **Servings:** 6

Ingredients

- 1 -1 1/2 lb country-style pork ribs, boneless
- 1 medium onion, chopped
- 1 (29 ounce) cans white hominy, drained (Posole)
- 1 (14 1/2 ounce) cans diced tomatoes
- 2 -3 cups chicken stock
- 2 garlic cloves, minced
- 1 (4 ounce) cans chopped green chili peppers
- 1 teaspoon salt
- 1/2 teaspoon thyme
- 1/4 teaspoon cumin

Directions

1. Brown pork ribs in a lightly oiled skillet.

2. Sauté onion and drain fat.Mix pork, onion and other ingredients in a crock pot.
3. Cook for 5 hours to 6 hours on low heat.

CROCK POT APRICOT CHICKEN

- **Prep Time:** 20 mins
- **Total Time:** 8 hrs 20 mins
- **Servings:** 4-6

Ingredients

- 1/2 cup French dressing
- 1/2 cup apricot jam
- 1 (1 1/2 ounce) packets dry onion soup mix
- 3 lbs skinless chicken pieces

Directions

1. Whisk together soup mix, dressing and jam in a bowl.
2. Cover the chicken pieces with this sauce and place in slow cooker.
3. Put the lid on and cook for 6 to 8 hours on Low or for 3 to 4 hours on High.

CROCK POT GREEN BEANS

- **Prep Time:** 10 mins
- **Total Time:** 8 hrs 10 mins
- **Servings:** 4-6

Ingredients

- 4 (14 1/2 ounce) cans green beans, drained
- 2 (14 ounce) cans chicken broth, seasoned with roasted garlic
- 1 onion, cleaned and cut into 6 wedges
- 1/2 lb bacon, cut into small pieces and semi fried
- bacon drippings
- salt, to taste
- pepper, to taste

Directions

1. Mix everything in a crock pot.
2. Cook for 8 hours on low or for 5 hours on high.

COUNTRY STYLE RIBS

- **Prep Time:** 10 mins
- **Total Time:** 6 hrs 10 mins

- **Servings:** 4-6

Ingredients

- 4 -5 lbs country-style pork ribs
- 1 (18 ounce) bottles of your favorite barbecue sauce (I used brown sugar flavor)
- 1 onion, chopped
- salt and pepper, to taste

Directions

1. Mix all ingredients in crock pot.
2. Cook for 6 to 8 hours on low.

SLOW COOKER ENCHILADA CASSEROLE

- **Prep Time:** 15 mins
- **Total Time:** 6 hrs 15 mins
- **Servings:** 4-6

Ingredients

- 1 1/2 lbs ground beef
- 1 medium onion, chopped
- 1 -2 garlic clove, minced
- 1/2 teaspoon salt
- 1/2 teaspoon pepper

- 6 corn tortillas
- 2 cups fresh corn (or 2 cups frozen corn or 15-oz can)
- 1 (19 ounce) cans enchilada sauce
- 2 cups shredded cheddar cheese
- 1 (2 1/2 ounce) cans sliced ripe olives, drained
- 1 cup sour cream

Directions

1. Brown the ground beef in an oiled skillet and remove separately. Add onion and garlic to make them transparent.
2. Mix with beef, the onion and garlic and salt and pepper. In bottom of crock pot place 2 tortillas. Put 1/3rd of meat, sauce, corn, olives and cheese. Repeat process two times.
3. Put the lid and cook for 6-8 hours on low. Serve with sour cream.

CROCK POT RIGATONI

- **prep Time:** 20 mins
- **Total Time:** 4 hrs 20 mins
- **Servings:** 8

Ingredients

- 28 ounces spaghetti sauce, jarred or home-made
- 12 ounces rigatoni pasta, cooked
- 1 1/2 lbs ground beef or 1 1/2 lbs sausage, browned
- 3 cups shredded mozzarella cheese
- 1/2-3/4 lb sliced pepperoni
- sliced mushrooms (optional)
- onion (optional)

Directions

1. Make two layers of the ingredients one after the other.
2. Cover and cook for 4-5 hours on low.

CROCK POT APPLESAUCE

- **Prep Time:** 25 mins
- **Total Time:** 3 hrs 25 mins
- **Yield:** 6 cups

Ingredients

- 4 lbs tart apples, cored and sliced thin
- 1/2 cup sugar
- 1/2 teaspoon cinnamon
- 1 cup water

o   1 tablespoon lemon juice

Directions

1. Mix apples, sugar and cinnamon into a crock pot.
2. Pour water and lemon juice to cover them.
3. Cook for 6 hours on low or for 3 hours on high.

JAPANESE BEEF STEW

- **Prep Time:** 5 mins
- **Total Time:** 12 hrs 5 mins
- **Servings:** 6

Ingredients

- 2 lbs beef stew meat
- 1 cup water
- 1/2 cup Japanese sake (dry white wine)
- 1/4 cup sugar
- 1/4 cup soy sauce
- 1 teaspoon salt
- 1/2 lb baby carrots
- 3 medium potatoes, peeled and chopped
- 1 white onion, diced

Directions

1. Put everything in a crock pot.
2. Cook for 10-12 hours on low or for 4-6 hours on high.

CROCK POT BEAN DIP

- **Prep Time:** 0 mins
- **Total Time:** 2 hrs
- **Servings:** 1

Ingredients

- 1 (15 ounce) cans refried beans
- 1 cup picante sauce (your choice)
- 1 cup shredded monterey jack cheese
- 1 cup shredded cheddar cheese
- 3/4 cup sour cream
- 1 (3 ounce) packages cream cheese, softened
- 1 tablespoon chili powder
- 1/4 teaspoon ground cumin
- tortilla chips
- salsa

Directions

1. Mix first 8 ingredients in a slow cooker.
2. Put the lid on and cook for 2 hours on high.

3. Stir once or twice. Serve with chips and salsa.

CROCK POT BAKED BEANS BANANZA

- **Prep Time:** 10 mins
- **Total Time:** 5 hrs 10 mins
- **Yield:** 1 crockpot

Ingredients

- 1 (15 ounce) cans pork and beans
- 1 (15 ounce) cans lima beans
- 1 (15 ounce) cans garbanzo beans
- 1 (15 ounce) cans kidney beans
- 1/2 lb ground beef, cooked and crumbled
- 1/2 lb bacon, cooked slightly
- 1/2 cup ketchup
- 2 teaspoons mustard
- 1 1/2 tablespoons vinegar
- 2 teaspoons salt
- 3/4 cup brown sugar
- 1 cup chili sauce
- 1 onion, diced

Directions

1. Put everything in a crock pot and cook for 5-6 hours on low or for 2-3 hours on high.

CROCK-POT MACARONI AND CHEESE

- **Prep Time:** 20 mins
- **Total Time:** 4 hrs 20 mins
- **Servings:** 6-8

Ingredients

- 1 (16 ounce) packages macaroni, any type
- 1 tablespoon oil
- 1 (14 ounce) cans evaporated milk
- 1 1/2 cups milk
- 1 teaspoon salt
- 3 cups shredded cheddar cheese (sharp is what she uses)
- 1/2 cup melted butter

Directions

1. Lightly grease crock pot and put cooked macaroni in it with a little oil.
2. Add remaining ingredients and stir.
3. Put the lid and cook on low for 3-4 hours.

DRUNKEN MEATBALLS

- **Prep Time:** 5 mins
- **Total Time:** 55 mins
- **Yield:** 48 meatballs

Ingredients

- 1 cup brown sugar
- 1 cup ketchup
- 1/2 cup Bourbon
- 4 dozen meatballs, small, already cooked

Directions

1. Mix the first three ingredients. Cook on simmer for 5 minute.
2. Add meatballs and cook for another 45 minutes with cover.
3. Make the sauce in the above mentioned process. Put meatballs and sauce into crock pot and cook for 8 to 12 hours on low.

CROCK POT CRANBERRY CHICKEN

- **Prep Time:** 15 mins
- **Total Time:** 8 hrs 15 mins
- **Servings:** 4-6

Ingredients

- 1 cup sliced onion
- 12 skinless chicken thighs
- 1 cup whole berry cranberry sauce
- 1 tablespoon low-sodium beef bouillon cube
- 1 teaspoon apple cider vinegar
- 1 teaspoon prepared mustard
- 1 1/2 teaspoons salt

Directions

1. Put the onions at the bottom of the slow cooker and arrange thighs over the onion.
2. Mix remaining ingredients together and coat the chicken with this.
3. Put the lid on and cook for 6 to 8 hours on Low or for 3 to 4 hours on High.

SLOW COOKER CHICKEN DINNER

- **Prep Time:** 15 mins
- **Total Time:** 9 hrs 15 mins
- **Servings:** 4

Ingredients

- 1 whole frying chicken, rinsed,giblets removed

- 8 large carrots, peeled and cut into 2 inch pieces
- 6 potatoes, peeled
- 1 package dry onion soup mix
- 1 teaspoon basil
- 1 cup chicken broth or 1 cup dry white wine

Directions

1. Put the chicken, potatoes and carrots in a slow cooker.
2. Mix other ingredients together and place over chicken.
3. Cook for 5 hours on high or for about 9 hours on low.

TURKEY LEG POT ROAST

- **Prep Time:** 15 mins
- **Total Time:** 5 hrs 15 mins
- **Servings:** 3-4

Ingredients

- 3 medium potatoes, peeled and quartered
- 2 cups baby carrots

- 2 celery ribs, cut into 2 1/2 inch pieces
- 1 medium onion, peeled and quartered
- 3 garlic cloves, peeled and quartered
- 1/2 cup fat-free low-sodium chicken broth
- 3 turkey drumsticks (about 1/2 lb each)
- 2 teaspoons seasoning salt
- 1 teaspoon dried thyme
- 1 teaspoon dried parsley
- 1/4 teaspoon pepper

Directions

1. Mix vegetables and broth in a greased oval 5-6 quart slow cooker.
2. Place drumsticks on this with remaining ingredients sprinkled over.
3. Put the lid on and cook for 5-5 1/2 hours on low.

CROCK POT PORK LOIN

- **Prep Time:** 5 mins
- **Total Time:** 6 hrs 5 mins
- **Servings:** 6-8

Ingredients

- 2 -3 lbs boneless pork loin or 2 -3 lbs pork tenderloin
- 3 tablespoons lemon juice
- 3 garlic cloves, mined
- 1 teaspoon crushed rosemary
- 1 teaspoon parsley flakes
- 1/2 teaspoon thyme
- 1/4 teaspoon pepper
- 1/4 teaspoon salt

Directions

1. Place raw pork in a slow cooker or crock pot.
2. Coat the pork well with all other ingredients.
3. Put the lid on and cook for 4-6 hours on high or for 6-8 hours on low.

EASY POTATO AND CORN CHOWDER

- **Prep Time:** 5 mins
- **Total Time:** 6 hrs 5 mins
- **Servings:** 6

Ingredients

- 1 (16 ounce) bags frozen hash brown potatoes, thawed

- 1 (15 1/4 ounce) cans whole kernel corn, undrained
- 1 (14 3/4 ounce) cans cream-style corn
- 1 (12 ounce) cans evaporated milk
- 1 medium onion, chopped
- 8 slices bacon, cooked and crumbled
- 1/2 teaspoon salt
- 1/2 teaspoon Worcestershire sauce
- 1/4 teaspoon pepper

Directions

1. Mix everything together in crock pot.
2. Cook on low for 6-8 hours.
3. Serve with a little shredded cheese and crumbled bacon on top of the serving bowl.

PEPPERONCINI CROCK POT BEEF

- **Prep Time:** 10 mins
- **Total Time:** 6 hrs 10 mins
- **Servings:** 12

Ingredients

- 1 (3 lb) beef chuck roast, trimmed of most fat
- 2 garlic cloves, sliced

- 1 (16 ounce) jars pepperoncini peppers (stems removed after cooking if using whole peppers)

Directions

1. Insert garlic slices in the roast by making cuts.
2. Put it in the slow cooker.
3. Empty contents of pepperoncini jar over meat. Put lid on and cook for 6 to 8 hours on LOW.

BAKED CINNAMON APPLES

- **Prep Time:** 30 mins
- **Total Time:** 2 hrs 30 mins
- **Servings:** 4-6

Ingredients

- 6 large very tart apples, cored, sliced and peeled (peels on is okay too!)
- 1 cup golden raisin
- 1 cup granulated sugar (or less if you have sweeter apples)
- 1/4 cup light brown sugar, packed
- 1 tablespoon cinnamon
- 1/8 teaspoon nutmeg
- 3 tablespoons cornstarch

- 4 tablespoons butter, sliced

Directions

1. Mix all ingredients into crock pot except butter.
2. Coat apple slices in this. Put butter on top.
3. Cook for 1-1/2 to 2 hours on HIGH OR for 3-1/2 to 4 hours cook on LOW. Stir only once in halfway.

MUSHROOM PORK TENDERLOIN

- **Prep Time:** 5 mins
- **Total Time:** 5 hrs 5 mins
- **Servings:** 6-8

Ingredients

- 2 pork tenderloin (1 pound each)
- 8 ounces fresh mushrooms, sliced
- 1 (10 3/4 ounce) cans condensed cream of onion soup, undiluted
- 1 (10 3/4 ounce) cans condensed golden mushroom soup, undiluted
- 1 (10 1/2 ounce) cans condensed French onion soup, undiluted

Directions

1. In a 3-qt. slow cooker, put pork and mushrooms.
2. Mix soups and pour over pork and mushrooms.
3. Put the lid and cook for 4-5 hours on low.When meat is tender, serve with mashed potatoes.

CROCK POT CHICKEN PAPRIKA

Ingredients

- 8 boneless skinless chicken breasts, cut in half
- 4 cups sliced thin potatoes
- 4 cups sliced thin onions
- 3 tablespoons virgin olive oil
- paprika
- salt & pepper
- 1 cup chicken broth

Directions

1. Make a bed of onion, potatoes.
2. Place the chicken, sprinkled with salt& pepper, paprika.
3. Drizzle oil on top.Add the broth and cook for 6-8 hours on low.

SLOW-COOKER STEAK CHILI

- **Prep Time:** 30 mins
- **Total Time:** 8 hrs 30 mins
- **Servings:** 8

Ingredients

- 2 tablespoons oil
- 2 lbs beef round steak, cut into 1-inch cubes
- 1 1/2 cups onions, chopped
- 2 garlic cloves, minced
- 1 1/3 cups water, divided
- 1 cup celery, chopped
- 2 (15 ounce) cans kidney beans, drained and rinsed
- 2 (14 1/2 ounce) cans diced tomatoes
- 1 (16 ounce) jars salsa
- 1 (15 ounce) cans tomato sauce
- 1 1/2 tablespoons chili powder
- 1 teaspoon ground cumin
- 1 teaspoon dried oregano
- 1/2 teaspoon pepper
- 2 tablespoons all-purpose flour
- 2 tablespoons cornmeal

Garnish

- diced tomatoes, sour cream, crushed tortilla chips or shredded cheddar cheese

Directions

1. In a sauté pan cook steak, onion and garlic over medium heat.When onion and garlic are translucent and steak is browned, transfer it to a slow cooker. Leave the juices.
2. Add salsa, celery, beans, one cup water, and tomatoes with juice, tomato sauce and seasonings.Put the lid and cook for 8 hours on low setting.
3. Make gravy with the juices in pan by whisking cornmeal, flour and remaining 1/3 cup water. Serve when thickened.

HAMBURGER VEGETABLE SOUP - CROCK POT

- **Prep Time:** 15 mins
- **Total Time:** 6 hrs 15 mins
- **Servings:** 6

Ingredients

- 8 ounces ground beef, cooked and drained
- 1 onion, diced

- 1 green pepper, diced
- 2 (15 ounce) cans diced tomatoes (with celery, green pepper and onion)
- 3 tablespoons ketchup
- 1 (14 1/2 ounce) cans beef broth
- 1 (16 ounce) bags frozen mixed vegetables (Classic mix with carrots, peas, green beans and corn)
- fresh ground pepper, to taste

Directions

1. Add everything in a crock pot.
2. Cook for 6-8 hours on Low.

CROCK POT TACO DIP

- **Prep Time:** 10 mins
- **Total Time:** 2 hrs 10 mins
- **Servings:** 6-8

Ingredients

- 1 teaspoon vegetable oil
- 1 lb ground chuck
- 1 (1 1/4 ounce) packages taco seasoning mix (I use Old El paso)

- 1 (10 ounce) jars medium salsa (I use Chi-Chi's brand)
- 1 lb Velveeta cheese, cubed
- 1 tablespoon sour cream
- 1/4 cup red onion, chopped
- 1 garlic clove, minced

Directions

1. Brown ground chuck in a skillet in a little oil. Sautés chopped onion and garlic. Drain fat.
2. Put meat mixture in crock pot with all other ingredients. Mix well and cook for 2-3 hours on low heat with lid on.
3. Stir once after the first hour. Garnish with green onion stems, finely chopped.

VEGETARIAN SLOW COOKER SPLIT PEA SOUP

- **Prep Time:** 10 mins
- **Total Time:** 4 hrs 10 mins
- **Serves:** 6-8, **Yield:** 8.0 cups

Ingredients

- 16 ounces split peas
- 4 medium carrots, peeled and diced
- 1 -1 1/2 cup white onion, chopped

- 2 garlic cloves, smashed
- 1 bay leaf
- 1 tablespoon salt
- 1/2 teaspoon pepper
- 6 cups hot water

Directions

1. Layer all the ingredients as in the list order without stirring.
2. Put the lid of the crock pot and cook 4-5 hours on High: or 8-10 hours on Low.
3. Remove bay leaf and garlic before serving.

CROCK POT CREAMY RANCH CHICKEN LIGHT

- **Prep Time:** 15 mins
- **Total Time:** 6 hrs 15 mins
- **Servings:** 4

Ingredients

- 4 boneless skinless chicken breasts
- 1 package hidden valley ranch dressing mix
- 8 ounces light sour cream
- 1 can low-fat cream of chicken soup
- 1/2 chopped yellow onion

- 1/2 cup water
- 1 pinch salt
- pepper

Directions

1. Mix everything in a crock pot.
2. Cook for 6 hours on low stirring occasionally.

EASY CROCK POT BBQ CHICKEN (LOW FAT)

- **Prep Time:** 5 mins
- **Total Time:** 8 hrs 5 mins
- **Servings:** 4

Ingredients

- 4 boneless skinless chicken breasts
- 1 1/2 cups barbecue sauce
- 1 red onion, diced

Directions

1. Mix everything in a crock pot and cook for 6-8 hours on low or for 4-6 hours on high.

Tangy Slow Cooker Pork Roast

- **Prep Time:** 10 mins
- **Total Time:** 7 hrs 10 mins
- **Servings:** 8

Ingredients

- 1 large onion, sliced
- 2 1/2 lbs boneless pork loin roast
- 1 cup hot water
- 1/4 cup white sugar
- 3 tablespoons red wine vinegar
- 2 tablespoons soy sauce
- 1 tablespoon ketchup
- 1/2 teaspoon ground black pepper
- 1/2 teaspoon salt
- 1/4 teaspoon garlic powder
- 1 dash hot pepper sauce (to taste)

Directions

1. Arrange onion slices at the bottom of the slow cooker and place the roast on top.
2. Mix sugar, water, vinegar, ketchup, garlic powder, soy sauce, salt, black pepper and hot sauce and pour over the roast.
3. Put the lid and cook for one hour on high at first and then for 4-6 hours on low.

BEEF & BAKED BEANS STEW

- **Prep Time:** 10 mins
- **Total Time:** 10 hrs 10 mins
- **Servings:** 6

Ingredients

- 1 1/4 lbs beef stew meat
- 4 unpeeled potatoes, cut into 1 inch cubes
- 1/2 cup chopped onion
- 1 teaspoon salt
- 1/4 teaspoon pepper
- 1 (28 ounce) cans baked beans (in bbq sauce)

Directions

1. Mix potatoes, salt and pepper, stew meat, onions in crock pot.
2. Spread beans over this meat mix.
3. Put the lid on and cook for 8-10 hours on low heat.

CROCK POT BREAKFAST APPLE COBBLER

- **prep Time:** 15 mins
- **Total Time:** 9 hrs 15 mins
- **Servings:** 2

Ingredients

- 4 medium apples, peeled and sliced (about 2 cups)
- 1/4 cup honey
- 1 teaspoon cinnamon
- 2 tablespoons butter, melted
- 2 cups granola cereal

Directions

1. Mix all ingredients together in a crock pot.
2. Put lid on and cook for 7 to 9 hours on low or for 2 to 3 hours on high.
3. Serve with milk.

SLOW COOKER LASAGNA

- **Prep Time:** 0 mins
- **Total Time:** 6 hrs
- **Servings:** 4-6

Ingredients

- 1 (16 ounce) boxes rigatoni pasta, cooked
- 1 1/2 lbs hamburger, browned and drained
- 1 green pepper, chopped
- 4 cups mozzarella cheese, shredded
- 2 cups cheddar cheese, shredded
- 2 (15 ounce) cans pizza sauce
- 1 tablespoon minced onion

Directions

1. Mix everything together and place in slow cooker.
2. Layer the lasagna in the traditional way if you want.
3. Cook for 5 hours on low.

CROCK POT PEPPERONI PIZZA DIP

- **Prep Time:** 15 mins
- **Total Time:** 3 hrs 15 mins
- **Servings:** 14

Ingredients

- 1 (14 ounce) jars pizza sauce

- 1 (6 ounce) packages pepperoni, sliced, chopped
- 8 medium green onions, chopped
- 1/2 cup red bell pepper, chopped
- 1 (2 1/4 ounce) cans black olives, sliced and drained
- 1 cup mozzarella cheese, shredded
- 1 (8 ounce) packages cream cheese, softened and cubed

Directions

1. Mix pepperoni, pizza sauce, bell pepper, olives and onions in a 1 1/2-quart slow cooker.
2. Put the lid and cook for 3-4 hours on LOW setting.
3. Add the cream cheese and mozzarella at the end.

CROCK POT CLAM CHOWDER

- **Prep Time:** 5 mins
- **Total Time:** 6 hrs 5 mins
- **Servings:** 10

Ingredients

- 1 (10 3/4 ounce) cans condensed cream of celery soup
- 1 (10 3/4 ounce) cans condensed cream of potato soup

- 1 (10 3/4 ounce) cans New England clam chowder
- 2 (6 1/2 ounce) cans minced clams
- 1 quart half-and-half cream
- 1 pint heavy whipping cream

Directions

1. Mix cream of potato soup, cream of celery soup, half-and-half cream, 1 can drained clams, 1 can un-drained clams, clam chowder, and whipping cream into a slow cooker.
2. Put the lid and cook for 6 to 8 hours on low.

CABBAGE AND SAUSAGE CROCK POT

- **Prep Time:** 15 mins
- **Total Time:** 23 mins
- **Servings:** 4-6

Ingredients

- 1 large onion, chopped
- 1 tablespoon butter
- 1 lb Italian sausage, sliced into 1 inch rounds (you can also use Kielbasa your favorite spicy sausage)
- 1 head cabbage, chopped (bite-size chunks)

- 1 (28 ounce) cans diced tomatoes
- 1 (10 3/4 ounce) cans cheddar cheese soup
- 1 cup beef broth

Directions

1. Layer all the ingredients in the listed order.
2. Cook for 4 to 6 hours on high or for 8 to 10 hours on low.

CROCK POT BEEF STEW

- **Prep Time:** 10 mins
- **Total Time:** 9 hrs 10 mins
- **Servings:** 6

Ingredients

- 1 1/2 lbs beef stew meat, cubed
- 1 onion, chunks
- 5 potatoes, chunks
- 4 carrots, 1 inch pieces
- 4 stalks celery, 1 inch pieces
- 1 (14 ounce) cans stewed tomatoes
- 3 1/2 cups water
- 2 beef bouillon cubes
- 2 vegetable bouillon cubes
- 1 tablespoon minced garlic

- 2 tablespoons cornstarch

Directions

1. Place the meat and other ingredients in a crock pot.
2. Cook for 9-10 hours on low.

VEGETABLE-BEEF BARLEY SOUP

- **Prep Time:** 20 mins
- **Total Time:** 8 hrs 20 mins
- **Servings:** 10

Ingredients

- 1 1/2 lbs lean stewing beef
- 1/2 cup bell pepper, chopped
- 1 (16 ounce) packages frozen mixed vegetables (I use a gumbo blend.)
- 3/4 cup chopped onion
- 2/3 cup uncooked barley
- 2 1/2 cups water
- 1 teaspoon salt
- 1/2 teaspoon dried thyme leaves
- 1/4 teaspoon pepper
- 1/2 teaspoon garlic powder
- 2 teaspoons beef bouillon

- 2 (14 1/2 ounce) cans diced tomatoes
- 1 (8 ounce) cans tomato sauce

Directions

1. Rinse and thaw frozen vegetables and add to the soup.
2. Mix everything in a 3 1/2- to 6-quart crock pot.
3. Put the lid on and cook for 8 hours on low heat.

CROCK POT CHICKEN CACCIATORE

- **Prep Time:** 5 mins
- **Total Time:** 3 hrs 5 mins
- **Servings:** 4-8

Ingredients

- 4 -6 lbs chicken thighs (skin on or off)
- 1 (28 ounce) cans crushed tomatoes (basil and garlic flavor)
- 1 tablespoon italian seasoning
- 1 tablespoon salt
- 1 teaspoon black pepper

Directions

1. Throw everything in the crock pot except the chicken.Stir well.
2. Now add the chicken.
3. Cook until chicken easily comes off bone, either on low or high heat.

CROCK POT CHICKEN VEGETABLE SOUP

- **prep Time:** 20 mins
- **Total Time:** 8 hrs 20 mins
- **Servings:** 6

Ingredients

- 2 cups chopped chicken (cooked or raw, I like to use raw)
- 2 tablespoons butter
- 3/4 cup chopped onion
- 1 cup chopped celery
- 1 tablespoon minced garlic
- 7 cups chicken broth
- 2 chicken bouillon cubes
- 1/2 teaspoon thyme
- 1 teaspoon oregano
- 1/2 teaspoon pepper
- 1 cup diced carrot
- 1 (15 1/4 ounce) cans sweet corn

Directions

1. Put everything in a crock pot.
2. Cook for 6 to 8 hours on high.

CROCK POT ROAST

- **Prep Time:** 10 mins
- **Total Time:** 7 hrs 10 mins
- **Servings:** 6-8

Ingredients

- 2 -3 lbs arm roast or 2 -3 lbs beef shoulder
- 1 1/4 ounces dry onion soup mix
- 3 cups water
- 4 -5 medium red potatoes, cubed
- 2 cups baby carrots

Directions

1. Combine beef shoulder, dry onion soup mix and water in a crock pot.
2. Cook for 7 hours on low or for 4.5 hours on high.
3. Add red potatoes and baby carrots before 45 minutes of serving.

Vegetarian meat Filling Substitute

- **Prep Time:** 10 mins
- **Total Time:** 8 hrs 10 mins
- **Servings:** 12

Ingredients

- 1 cup chopped onion
- 1 garlic clove, minced
- 1 teaspoon canola oil
- 1 cup dry lentils, rinsed
- 1 tablespoon chili powder
- 2 teaspoons ground cumin
- 1 teaspoon oregano
- 14 ounces water
- 2 vegetable bouillon cubes
- 1 cup salsa

Directions

1. Put all ingredients in the crock pot and cook for 8-12 hours on high.
2. Add water if needed.
3. Use as a meat taco filling.

CROCK POT CHICKEN FAJITAS

- **Prep Time:** 15 mins
- **Total Time:** 6 hrs 15 mins
- **Servings:** 6-8

Ingredients

- 1 1/2 lbs boneless chicken breasts, cut into strips
- 1 sweet vidalia onion, cut into thin wedges and separated
- 2 tablespoons lime juice
- 1 -2 garlic cloves, minced or 1 teaspoon garlic powder
- 3/4 teaspoon ground cumin
- 1 teaspoon seasoning salt
- 1/2 teaspoon chili powder
- 1 green bell pepper, thinly sliced (optional)
- 6 -8 flour tortillas, warmed
- shredded cheddar cheese (optional)
- salsa (optional)
- sour cream (optional)
- shredded lettuce (optional)

Directions

1. Place chicken and onions in a crock pot.

2. Sprinkle spices and lime juice and mix well.
3. Cook for 4-6 hours on low. If you are using frozen chicken breast, you need to cook more than 6 hours. Serve with warm tortillas and fajita toppings.

Slow Cooker Lentils

- **Prep Time:** 20 mins
- **Total Time:** 2 hrs 50 mins
- **Servings:** 10

Ingredients

- 1 3/4 cups lentils, sorted and rinsed
- 2 large onions, chopped
- 2 cloves garlic, minced
- 1 (14 1/2 ounce) cans diced tomatoes, with liquid
- 2 cups chicken broth
- 2 large carrots, sliced
- 1/2 cup sliced celery
- 1 bell pepper, diced
- 2 tablespoons chopped parsley
- 1 bay leaf
- 1/2 teaspoon salt
- 1/8 teaspoon marjoram
- 1/8 teaspoon sage

- 1/8 teaspoon thyme
- fresh ground pepper
- 1/2 lb low-fat cheddar cheese, shredded

Directions

1. Mix ingredients in the crock pot, except for the cheese and stir.
2. Cook for 2-1/2 hours on high setting.
3. Stir cheese before serving until it melts.

SWEET CROCK POT CHICKEN

- **Prep Time:** 5 mins
- **Total Time:** 6 hrs 5 mins
- **Serves:** 4, **Yield:** 4 pieces

Ingredients

- 4 bone-in chicken breast halves
- 1/2 cup water
- 1/2 cup packed brown sugar
- 1/2 cup ketchup
- 4 tablespoons white vinegar
- 4 tablespoons lemon juice
- 4 tablespoons Worcestershire sauce
- 1 small onion
- 1 tablespoon mustard

- 2 teaspoons paprika
- 2 teaspoons chili powder
- 1/2 teaspoon salt
- 1/8 teaspoon pepper

Directions

1. Mix ingredients except for the chicken in a crock pot.
2. Coat chicken with this sauce.
3. Cook for 6 1/2 hours on low.

CROCK POT PIZZA

- **Prep Time:** 15 mins
- **Total Time:** 2 hrs 15 mins
- **Serves:** 4-6, **Yield:** 4.0 1 cup servings

Ingredients

Crust

- 1 1/2 cups biscuit mix or 1 1/2 cups Bisquick, clone
- 1/2-3/4 cup water (Enough to make drop dumplings or form a sticky ball)

Sauce and Toppings

- 1 (16 ounce) jars pizza sauce or 2 cups homemade pizza sauce
- 1 -2 cup mozzarella cheese, depending on how much cheese you like
- pizza toppings, of your choice (precook and drain any raw meats)
- 2 tablespoons olive oil

Directions

1. Drizzle olive oil and put one quarter of pizza sauce at the bottom of the crock pot.
2. Mix Bisquick and water and spread on the sauce.
3. Top with cheese and meat and veggies.
4. Put the lid and cook for about 2 hours on high.

MEAT LOAF WITH SHIITAKE MUSHROOMS

- **Prep Time:** 10 mins
- **Total Time:** 5 hrs 10 mins
- **Servings:** 4-6

Ingredients

- 2 slices whole wheat bread
- 3/4 lb ground round
- 3/4 lb ground turkey
- 1 1/2 cups sliced shiitake mushrooms

- 1/2 cup grated fresh onion
- 1 teaspoon dried Italian seasoning
- 3/4 teaspoon salt
- 2 large eggs, lightly beaten
- 1 garlic clove, minced
- 2 tablespoons ketchup
- 1 1/2 teaspoons Dijon mustard
- 1/8 teaspoon ground red pepper

Directions

1. Make bread crumbs in food blender.
2. Combine beef with the crumbs, shiitake mushrooms, onion, dried Italian seasoning, salt, eggs and garlic. Shape this into a 9 x 6-inch loaf. Put loaf in an electric slow cooker.
3. Mix mustard, ketchup and pepper and coat the loaf with this mix. Cover and cook for 5 hours on LOW.

CROCK POT SPINACH SPECIAL

- **Prep Time:** 10 mins
- **Total Time:** 4 hrs 10 mins
- **Servings:** 8

Ingredients

- 3 (10 ounce) boxes frozen spinach (thawed and drained)
- 2 cups cottage cheese
- 1 1/2 cups cheddar cheese, grated
- 3 eggs
- 1/4 cup flour
- 1 teaspoon salt
- 3 tablespoons butter or 3 tablespoons margarine, melted

Directions

1. Mix everything in a large bowl and put into a crock pot.
2. Cook on High for 1 hour and then for 3 more hours on low.

TOMATO SOUP WITH ISRAELI COUSCOUS

- **Prep Time:** 10 mins
- **Total Time:** 6 hrs 10 mins
- **Servings:** 4

Ingredients

- 1 tablespoon olive oil
- 1 medium yellow onion, chopped
- 1 garlic clove, minced

- 3 cups vegetable stock
- 1 (28 ounce) cans crushed tomatoes
- 1 tablespoon tomato paste
- 1 pinch sugar (or a natural sweetener)
- 2 bay leaves
- salt
- fresh ground black pepper
- 1 cup cooked israeli couscous
- 2 tablespoons chopped fresh basil leaves (to garnish)

Directions

1. Sauté onion and garlic in a medium-size skillet with little oil over medium heat.
2. Put vegetables in a 4-quart slow cooker. Add tomatoes, sugar, bay leaves, stock, tomato paste and salt and pepper. Cover with lid and cook for 5-8 hours on low.
3. Serve with couscous with basil sprinkled on top of the bowl.

VEGETARIAN CHIPOTLE CHILI

- **Prep Time:** 15 mins
- **Total Time:** 6 hrs 15 mins
- **Servings:** 4

Ingredients

- 1 (15 ounce) cans black beans, drained and rinsed (or 1 1/2 - 2 cups cooked beans)
- 1 (15 ounce) cans navy beans, drained and rinsed (or 1 1/2 - 2 cups cooked beans)
- 1 (14 1/2 ounce) cans diced tomatoes
- 1 (14 1/2 ounce) cans diced tomatoes and green chilies or 1 (14 1/2 ounce) cans diced tomatoes with jalapenos
- 1 cup onion, chopped
- 6 garlic cloves, minced
- 2 tablespoons chili powder
- 1 tablespoon sweet Hungarian paprika
- 1 tablespoon dried cilantro (optional)
- 1/2 teaspoon fresh coarse ground black pepper
- 1 teaspoon chipotle chile, minced

Directions

1. Mix everything in a large slow cooker or 4 1/2 quart.
2. Cook for 6 hours on low heat.
3. Serve with sour cream or cheese.

TOMATO SPINACH SLOW COOKER SOUP

- **Prep Time:** 5 mins
- **Total Time:** 5 hrs 5 mins
- **Servings:** 8

Ingredients

- 10 ounces Baby Spinach, washed
- 2 medium carrots, chopped
- 2 medium celery ribs, chopped
- 1 large onion, chopped
- 1 garlic clove, minced
- 4 cups low sodium vegetable broth
- 1 (28 ounce) diced tomatoes
- 2 leaves bay leaves
- 1 tablespoon dried basil
- 1 teaspoon dried oregano
- 1/2 teaspoon red pepper flakes, crushed

Directions

1. Mix everything in a slow cooker.
2. Put the lid on and cook for 5 hours on high or for 8-10 hours on low.
3. Remove bay leaves and serve.

BROCCOLI CHEESE SOUP FOR THE CROCK POT

- **Prep Time:** 10 mins

- **Total Time:** 3 hrs 10 mins
- **Serves:** 4-6, **Yield:** 4.0 bowls of soup

Ingredients

- 1/2 cup green pepper, chopped
- 1/2 cup onion, chopped
- 2 tablespoons butter or 2 tablespoons margarine
- 1 (10 ounce) cans cream of chicken soup
- 1 1/2 cups milk
- 1 lb Velveeta cheese, cubed
- 1 (10 ounce) packages frozen chopped broccoli

Directions

1. Sauté green pepper and onion in butter.
2. Mix everything in a crock pot and cook for 3-4 hours in low heat. Make sure not to add salt.

CROCK POT CREAMY CHICKEN

- **Prep Time:** 10 mins
- **Total Time:** 6 hrs 10 mins
- **Servings:** 8

Ingredients

- 8 chicken thighs
- 8 red potatoes, quartered
- 1 (5 ounce) cans mushrooms
- 2 (10 ounce) cans condensed cream of mushroom soup
- 2 cups milk
- 4 cups water
- 1 tablespoon minced onion

Directions

1. Put everything in a crock pot or slow cooker.
2. Cook until chicken falls off the bone or potatoes are tender or for about 6 hours.
3. Add salt and pepper to taste.

EASY CROCK POT MEATBALLS

- **Prep Time:** 15 mins
- **Total Time:** 4 hrs 15 mins
- **Serves:** 4, **Yield:** 4 servings per pound of meatballs

Ingredients

- 1 (10 3/4 ounce) cans condensed tomato soup
- 2 tablespoons brown sugar
- 1 tablespoon vinegar

- 1 tablespoon Worcestershire sauce
- 1 teaspoon prepared mustard
- 1/2 cup chopped onion
- 1/3 cup chopped green pepper
- butter, to saute
- 1 lb frozen meatballs

Directions

1. Add soup, Worcestershire sauce, vinegar, brown sugar and mustard to meatballs.
2. Sauté green peppers and onions in butter.
3. Mix this with the sauce. Cook for 4 to 6 hours on low.

CROCK POT MELT

- **Prep Time:** 2 mins
- **Total Time:** 8 hrs 2 mins
- **Servings:** 4-6

Ingredients

- 5 -6 cube steaks
- 2 (10 3/4 ounce) cans Campbell's Cream of Mushroom Soup
- 1 (1 1/4 ounce) packets dry onion soup mix
- 1/2 cup water

Directions

1. Mix cubed steaks, dry onion soup, cream of mushroom soup and water together in a crock pot.
2. Cook for 8-10 hours on low or until steaks are tender.

CROCK POT BLUEBERRY DUMP CAKE

- **Prep Time:** 10 mins
- **Total Time:** 2 hrs 10 mins
- **Servings:** 4

Ingredients

- 1 (21 ounce) cans blueberry pie filling
- 1 (18 1/4 ounce) packages yellow cake mix
- 1/2 cup butter
- 1/2 cup walnuts, chopped

Directions

1. Mix pie filling, butter and dry cake mix together in a slow cooker.
2. Sprinkle walnuts on top of that.Put the lid on and cook for 2 to 3 hours on low.

3. Serve warm with vanilla ice cream or whipped cream in bowls.

SPLIT PEA AND PARSNIP SOUP

- **prep Time:** 10 mins
- **Total Time:** 8 hrs 10 mins
- **Servings:** 4-6

Ingredients

- 1 tablespoon olive oil
- 1 medium yellow onion, chopped
- 2 large parsnips, peeled and halved lengthwise and cut into thin half moons
- 1 lb dried split peas, picked over and rinsed
- 1 teaspoon dried thyme
- 1 bay leaf
- 6 cups vegetable stock
- 1 teaspoon salt (or to taste depending on your stock)
- fresh ground black pepper
- 1 teaspoon liquid smoke (optional)

Directions

1. Sauté onion and parsnips, in a large skillet with little oil over medium heat. Shift them to a 4-6 quart slow cooker.

2. Put the thyme, bay leaf, peas and the stock.Put the lid and cook for eight hours on low or until the peas disappear.
3. Add salt and pepper to taste.Discard the bay leaf and add the liquid smoke.

CROCK POT LENTIL AND SAUSAGE SOUP

- **Prep Time:** 10 mins
- **Total Time:** 6 hrs 10 mins
- **Servings:** 8

Ingredients

- 1 cup uncooked lentils
- 1/2 lb kielbasa, cut into 1 inch pieces
- 1 cup onion, chopped
- 1 cup celery, chopped
- 1 cup carrot, finely chopped
- 1 cup potato, diced
- 2 tablespoons chopped fresh parsley
- 3 (16 ounce) cans beef broth
- 1/2 teaspoon fresh ground black pepper
- 1/8 teaspoon nutmeg

Directions

1. Wash, drain water and rinse lentils.

2. Put everything in a crock pot.
3. Cook for 6 hours on low.Keep stirring occasionally.

CROCK POT ROAST

- **Prep Time:** 5 mins
- **Total Time:** 8 hrs 5 mins
- **Servings:** 6

Ingredients

- 1 (10 3/4 ounce) cans cream of mushroom soup
- 1 (10 3/4 ounce) cans cream of celery soup
- 1 (1 ounce) package dry onion soup mix
- 1 (10 3/4 ounce) cans water
- 1 roast (I use pork, but can use any type meat)

Directions

1. Mix everything in a crock pot.
2. Cook for 8 hours on low.

PINTO BEANS WITH HAM

- **Prep Time:** 5 mins
- **Total Time:** 8 hrs 5 mins
- **Servings:** 6-8

Ingredients

- 1 lb dried pinto bean, sorted and washed
- 5 cups water
- 1 large onion, chopped
- 4 -8 ounces cooked ham, chopped
- 3 garlic cloves, minced
- 2 jalapeno peppers, seeded and chopped
- 1 tablespoon chili powder
- 1 teaspoon pepper
- 1/2 teaspoon ground cumin
- 1/4 teaspoon dried oregano
- salt, to taste

Directions

1. Soak beans in water, overnight and drain.Put beans in a 6 quart crock pot, rest of the ingredients except salt and water.Cook for 8-10 hours on low setting.
2. Add salt when beans are done. Salt will make the beans a bit tough.
3. Add jalapenos to give the beans a bit of heat. Add chopped green bell pepper if you do not want much heat.

Potato Crock Pot Recipe

- **Prep Time:** 10 mins
- **Total Time:** 3 hrs 10 mins
- **Servings:** 4-6

Ingredients

- 1 (10 3/4 ounce) cans cream of mushroom soup
- 1/2 teaspoon pepper
- 1/2 teaspoon paprika
- 1 cup shredded cheddar cheese (4 ounces)
- 4 medium baking potatoes, sliced 1/4-inch thick

Directions

1. Mix paprika, soup and pepper in a crock pot.
2. Add the potatoes in it with the cheese sprinkled on top.
3. Put the lid and cook for 3-4 hours on high.

Slow Cooker Cheddar Polenta

- **Prep Time:** 10 mins
- **Total Time:** 2 hrs 10 mins

- **Servings:** 8

Ingredients

- 7 cups hot water
- 2 cups polenta (not quick-cooking) or 2 cups coarse-ground yellow cornmeal
- 2 tablespoons extra virgin olive oil
- 2 teaspoons salt
- 1/2 teaspoon black pepper
- 3 cups grated extra-sharp cheddar cheese (about 12 ounces)

Directions

1. Mix polenta, water, olive oil, salt and pepper together in a slow cooker. Mix well. Add cheddar cheese to this and stir again. Cover with lid and cook for about 2 hours on high setting.
2. As polenta gets a thick consistency, add pour this to a buttered baking sheet. Cover with plastic wrap to let it cool.
3. Cut rectangular pieces and sauté them with olive oil in nonstick skillet until golden on both sides.

CROCK POT CHUCK ROAST

- **Prep Time:** 5 mins

- **Total Time:** 8 hrs 5 mins
- **Servings:** 4-6

Ingredients

- 4 lbs boneless chuck roast, cut up in pieces
- 1 (10 1/2 ounce) cans cream of mushroom soup
- 1/4 cup A.1. Original Sauce
- 1 (1 1/4 ounce) packages onion soup mix
- 3/4 cup water

Directions

1. Mix everything in a crock pot.
2. Cook for 8 hours on low.

EASY CROCK POT TERIYAKI CHICKEN

- **Prep Time:** 5 mins
- **Total Time:** 13 mins
- **Servings:** 3-4

Ingredients

- 6 -8 skinless chicken thighs
- 1/2 cup low sodium soy sauce
- 2 tablespoons brown sugar

- 2 tablespoons grated fresh ginger
- 2 garlic cloves, minced

Directions

1. Wash, rinse and pat dry chicken. Put it in a slow cooker.
2. Mix everything over the chicken.
3. Put the lid on and cook for 1 hour on high heat and then reduce the heat to low to cook for more 6-7 hours.

CROCK POT WHITE CHILI W/ CHICKEN

- **Prep Time:** 10 mins
- **Total Time:** 4 hrs 10 mins
- **Servings:** 6-8

Ingredients

- 3 (15 ounce) cans great northern beans, drained
- 8 ounces chicken breasts, diced into bite size pieces
- 1 cup onion, chopped
- 1 small green pepper, chopped
- 1 small red pepper, chopped
- 2 jalapenos, diced (or (to taste)

- 3 garlic cloves, minced
- 1 tablespoon ground cumin
- 1 teaspoon salt
- 1 tablespoon dried oregano
- 3 1/2 cups chicken broth

Directions

1. Mix everything in a crock pot.
2. Put the lid and cook for 8 hours on low or for 4 hours on high.

CROCK POT NC PULLED PORK

- **Prep Time:** 30 mins
- **Total Time:** 8 hrs 30 mins
- **Servings:** 6-8

Ingredients

- 2 onions, quartered
- 2 tablespoons brown sugar
- 1 tablespoon smoked paprika
- 2 teaspoons salt
- 1/2 teaspoon ground black pepper
- 1 (4 -6 lb) pork butt or 1 (4 -6 lb) shoulder roast
- **Sauce**

- 1 cup cider vinegar
- 1/3 cup Worcestershire sauce
- 1 1/2 teaspoons crushed red pepper flakes
- 2 teaspoons sugar
- 1/2 teaspoon dry mustard
- 1/2 teaspoon garlic salt
- 1/4 teaspoon cayenne pepper

Directions

1. Rub paprika, brown sugar, salt and pepper on the roast. Make a bed of onions in the crock pot.Mix Worcestershire sauce, vinegar, salt, mustard, red pepper flakes, sugar, cayenne pepper and garlic well. Drizzle 1/3 of this mix on the roast.
2. Refrigerate remaining mixture with a cover on it. Place the meat on the onions, and roast for 8-10 hours on low or 4 hours on high. Remove the roast and shred meat, discarding onions.
3. Mix remaining refrigerated vinegar mixture and the pot juices and serve with sandwiches.

CRANBERRY BARBECUE CHICKEN - CROCK POT

- **Prep Time:** 5 mins
- **Total Time:** 6 hrs 5 mins

- **Servings:** 6-8

Ingredients

- 3 -4 lbs chicken pieces
- 1/2 teaspoon salt
- 1/2 teaspoon pepper
- 1/2 cup celery, diced
- 1/2 cup onion, diced
- 1 (16 ounce) cans whole berry cranberry sauce
- 1 cup barbecue sauce

Directions

1. Mix everything in a slow cooker.
2. Put the lid on and bake for 4 hours on high or for 6-8 hours on low.
3. Thicken the sauce with corn starch or flour before serving.

CHICKEN STEW

- **Prep Time:** 10 mins
- **Total Time:** 40 mins
- **Servings:** 8

Ingredients

- 2 cups diced cooked chicken (boiled)
- 1 (16 ounce) cans whole kernel corn
- 1 (16 ounce) cans creamed corn
- 1 small onion, finely diced
- 1 (14 1/2 ounce) cans chicken broth (not the condensed kind)
- 1 (10 3/4 ounce) cans cream of chicken soup, so or 1 (10 3/4 ounce) cans cream of celery soup
- salt and pepper, as needed
- 2 -3 bay leaves
- 1 pinch basil
- 1/2 teaspoon fresh rosemary, snipped (optional)
- 3 tablespoons butter

Directions

1. Mix everything together in a crock pot.
2. Cook on for approximately 6 hours on low setting.
3. Serve with a green salad and saltine crackers.

CROCK POT APPLE AND SAUERKRAUT KIELBASA (LOW FAT)

- **Prep Time:** 5 mins
- **Total Time:** 4 hrs 5 mins

- **Servings:** 4

Ingredients

- 1 lb low-fat kielbasa, cut into chunks
- 2 medium apples, peeled and cut into small cubes
- 1 (14 ounce) cans sauerkraut
- 1 medium onion, chopped
- 2 tablespoons spicy mustard

Directions

1. Combine everything in a crock pot.
2. Cook 4-6 hours on high for.

CROCK POT MUSHROOM CHICKEN

- **Prep Time:** 10 mins
- **Total Time:** 5 hrs 10 mins
- **Servings:** 4

Ingredients

- 4 chicken breasts
- 1 (10 ounce) cream of mushroom soup
- 1 teaspoon hidden valley ranch dressing mix
- 1/4 cup milk
- 1/4 cup sour cream
- 2 small potatoes, sliced thin (optional)

Directions

1. Put chicken breasts in a crock pot.
2. Add potatoes to it. Mix dressing mix, soup and milk in a small bowl.
3. Pour this mix over chicken. Cook for 1 hour on high or for 3 to 4 hours on low. Add the sour cream before 15 minutes of serving.

SLOW COOKER CHICKEN POZOLE

- **Prep Time:** 10 mins
- **Total Time:** 5 hrs 10 mins
- **Servings:** 8

Ingredients

- 1 1/4 lbs boneless skinless chicken thighs, cut into 1 inch pieces
- 2 garlic cloves, finely chopped
- 2 (15 ounce) cans white hominy, drained and rinsed
- 1 medium onion, chopped
- 1 teaspoon dried oregano
- 1/2 teaspoon cumin
- 1/4 teaspoon dried red pepper flakes
- 2 chicken bouillon cubes
- 4 cups water

- 1 (14 1/2 ounce) cans diced tomatoes with green chilies (such as Rotel)
- 1 tablespoon lime juice
- 1/4 teaspoon salt
- 1/4 teaspoon pepper

Directions

1. Mix garlic, chicken, onion, hominy, cumin, bouillon cubes, oregano, red pepper flakes and water in a slow cooker.
2. Put the lid on and cook for 3 hours on high or for 5 hours on low.
3. Add lime juice, tomatoes, salt and pepper before serving and serve hot.

MAPLE SLOW COOKER BONELESS RIBS

- **Prep Time:** 5 mins
- **Total Time:** 8 hrs 5 mins
- **Servings:** 6

Ingredients

- 1 1/2 lbs boneless pork ribs
- 1/4 cup maple syrup
- 1/4 cup soy sauce
- 1 tablespoon Worcestershire sauce

- 2 tablespoons dried onion flakes
- 1 teaspoon ground cinnamon
- 1 teaspoon ground allspice
- 1 tablespoon minced garlic, about 6 cloves
- 1 tablespoon grated ginger
- 1 dash hot sauce
- ground black pepper

Directions

1. Rub pepper on the rubs. Put them in a slow cooker.
2. Mix all other ingredients in a small bowl and spread the sauce over the meat.
3. Cook for 6-8 hours on low or for 3-4 hours on high.

SLOW COOKER SPICED APPLESAUCE (CROCK POT)

- **Prep Time:** 10 mins
- **Total Time:** 8 hrs 10 mins
- **Servings:** 8-10

Ingredients

- 8 golden delicious apples, cored, peeled and cubed

- 1/2 cup brown sugar, packed
- 1/2 cup water
- 1 teaspoon pumpkin pie spice

Directions

1. Mix everything in a slow cooker.
2. Cover with lid and cook for 8 to 10 hours on low setting, or for 3 to 4 hours on high setting.
3. Add applesauce to get desired consistency.

SAUSAGE AND CABBAGE SOUP FOR THE CROCK-POT

- **Prep Time:** 15 mins
- **Total Time:** 5 hrs 15 mins
- **Servings:** 6-8

Ingredients

- 1 lb Polish sausage, smoked, halved lengthwise and chopped 3/4 inch
- 3 teaspoons extra virgin olive oil
- 6 cups chicken broth
- 2 cups water
- 1 head green cabbage, chopped
- 3 carrots, peeled and coarsely chopped
- 1 white onion, coarsely chopped

- 2 -3 garlic cloves, peeled
- 2 teaspoons caraway seeds
- 1 1/2 teaspoons italian seasoning
- 1 teaspoon celery salt
- 1 teaspoon garlic powder
- 1 teaspoon black pepper

Directions

1. Sauté chopped sausage with olive oil in a skillet over medium heat.
2. Add garlic, onion, carrots, cabbage, Italian seasoning, caraway seeds, salt, celery, broth and water to the crock pot.
3. Cook for two hours on high with occasional stirs. Add other ingredients and cook for three more hours.

CROCK POT LENTIL AND HAM SOUP

- **Prep Time:** 15 mins
- **Total Time:** 8 hrs 15 mins
- **Servings:** 6

Ingredients

- 2 cups lentils, uncooked
- 1 onion, chopped

- 2 celery ribs, chopped
- 2 carrots, sliced
- 1 bay leaf
- 1 (14 1/2 ounce) cans diced tomatoes, undrained
- 5 garlic cloves, minced
- 1/2 teaspoon salt
- 1/2 teaspoon pepper
- 1 sprig fresh thyme
- 1/4 teaspoon crushed red pepper flakes (optional)
- 1 lb smoked ham, cut into chunks
- 2 quarts water

Directions

1. Mix everything into a 6 quarter or larger crock pot.
2. Cover with lid and cook for 8-10 hours on low.
3. Discard thyme sprig and bay leaf and serve hot.

****

CONCLUSION

Thank you again for buy this book!

I hope this book was able to give you the flavor that you have been looking for in your Slow Cooker Simple to Follow Recipes.

The next step is to try the different recipes and share them with the people you hold dear.

Finally, if you enjoyed this book, please take the time to share your thoughts and post a review. It'd be greatly appreciated!

Thank you and good luck!

Did you enjoy this book?

I want to thank you for purchasing and reading this book. I really hope you got a lot out of it.

Can I ask a quick favor though?

If you enjoyed this book I would really appreciate it if you could leave me a positive review on Amazon.

I love getting feedback from my customers and reviews on Amazon really do make a difference. I read all my reviews and would really appreciate your thoughts.

Thanks so much.

Nancy Kelsey

Disclaimer

This Book, slow cooker recipes is written with an intention to serve as purely information and educational resource. It is not intended to be a medical advice or a medical guide.

Although proper care has been taken to ensure to validity and reliability of the information provided in this book. Readers are advice to exert caution before using any information, suggestion and methods described in this book.

The writer does not advocate the use of any of the suggestion, diet and health programs mention in this book. This book is not intended to take the place of a medical profession, a doctor and physician. The information in this book should not be used without the explicit advice from medically trained professions especially in cases where urgent diagnosis and medical treatment is needed.

The author or publisher cannot e held responsible for any personal or commercial damage in misinterpreting or misunderstanding any part of the book.

Printed in Great Britain
by Amazon